© Mervin Francis 2024
Life, Dreams, and Challenges

978-0-6398518-4-6 Paperback
978-0-6398518-5-3 eBook

Published by SAKURA BOOK PUBLISHING
- South Africa
alta@sakurabookpublishing.com

All rights reserved. No part of this publication may be reproduced, stored in a retrieval system, or transmitted in any form by any means electronic, mechanical, photocopying, recording or otherwise without the written permission of the copyright owner.

Printed in South Africa

ABOUT THE AUTHOR

Mervin M Francis unleashes his 3rd Anthology of Poetry. Starting out in his first book as a whimsical poet, Mervin evolved into writing positive poetry in his 2nd book. In his 3rd book Mervin dwells deeper into life's challenges and Dreams. Living in the North Coast of Durban, Mervin continues writing poetry in his free time whilst still holding a management role in Toyota SA. Mervin continues to write poetry, so that he can enjoy the freedom, of sharing his words, thoughts and emotions, with the rest of the world.

MERVIN M FRANCIS

A New Year

We waited for Christmas with great anticipation
We acknowledged Christ's birth with joyous celebrations
Now Christmas day has come and gone
But the joyful tidings that it brought still lingers on

The year has ended and a new one has begun
Have we conquered our challenges or left them undone
Are there unanswered questions as we start a New Year
Do we have a firm footing, is our path finally clear

Positive thoughts should fill your mind
For the New Year, leave all the negativity behind
Embrace what the world begins to throw your way
Be strong, stand firm and from your path never stray

Remember your mistakes from the years gone by
Use them so that you can spread your wings and fly
Use them to fight for what is dear
Use them as strength to take on new challenges this New Year.

Happy Anniversary

The most precious thing for me is having you in my life
And my journey got better when you agreed to be my wife
As the years pass by, beautiful memories we get to store
For this, I am more thankful than I ever was before

Our lives have changed in so many ways
The strength of our love in my heart forever will stay
You are the lighthouse that guides me through the darkest of night
Steering me away from danger by shining so bright

As we celebrate another wonderful year together
I want you to know that I will treasure you forever
Happy Anniversary to you with all my love
Thank you, Lord, for the endless blessings from above.

Life's Lessons

I watched as he passed me by
Nothing but sadness was etched in his eyes
A sudden feeling of uneasiness filled the air
As I looked at his demeanor and unkept hair

I called out to him hoping he would hear
Can I have a moment of your time please sir
He stopped, turned, and looked straight at me
My time is precious so speak up or let me be

I don't have the time for a lecture on life
I have been through it all, I have weathered my strife.
I stood in awe as he casually spoke
His tone was gentle, but his words were no joke

You see, life has taught me many things
Especially the hardship that destruction brings.
I reached out to you to show you that people still care
No matter your challenges you can still find humanity out there

We spoke for hours, and I learned a lot from him that day
From the simplicities of life to the mixed opportunities that comes our way
Never again will I allow seeds of doubt to be planted.
And never again will I take life for granted

Loved Ones Lost

It's never an easy thing to be able to understand how one is affected when loved ones are lost
But one thing rings true is that the pain that captures our hearts comes at a very high cost
There are those beautiful moments that were shared that runs rampant through our mind
We close our eyes hoping it's a dream and when we awaken our loved ones we will find

But that hope is distant for the truth is what stares us full in our face
Knowing that new memories will never be formed no, not here in this place
Now we need to embrace the days that are still to come
Days where we will need an abundance of strength to weather this storm

A storm that fills our hearts with endless emotions and unwanted pain
This tragedy has robbed us of sharing happiness again
Fear not for the heavens have gained new Angels and that I believe to be true
All I ask is to take solace in all the beautiful memories that was shared with you.

Place of Tranquility

The sun was out, and the sky was clear
I jumped in my car and threw it into gear
I stepped on the gas and headed straight for the beach
And within minutes of my destination, I did reach

I turned off the engine and looked all around
A place of tranquility is what I found
I stepped out of the car and locked the door
Then, I slowly made my way toward the seashore

As the warmth of the sun caressed my face
It brought me great joy just being in this place
I watched as the waves crashed and created a spray
I watched as the people continued on their merry way

I was envious of them for they made time to play
Whilst I made excuses to stay away
One look at the oceans and time stands still
And all emptiness within you can magically fill

Nature has blessed us with an amazing cure
A place of tranquility a place so pure
Make time to enjoy it come what may
Remember this place of tranquility is here forever to stay.

Rest Well My Friend
(In Memory of David Surajpal)

Rest well my friend as we get to honor your life today
With memories we've shared, which in our hearts
forever will stay
Although your journey on earth had reached its end
Your legacy lives on my dear friend

The time that we spent will always be cherished
And the love in our hearts will never perish
To your family, you are still the brightest star
That smiles down on them from the heavens afar

The joy that you spread wherever you went
The help you would give and the shoulder that you lent
And for making time to be part of everything, we did
We will forever be grateful for the part that you played

Rest well my friend in the arms of our heavenly father
Cherished times will linger on forever
We salute you and all that you did
Thank you, Lord, for the life that he lived.

Rest well my friend in the arms of the Lord
Rest well my friend and sing with one accord
For now, your memories are all that we get to keep
Rest well my friend until in heaven we shall meet.

Sounds of Nature

I woke up this morning to the sound of waves crashing.
To my ears, they were both soft and soothing
I got out of bed and ventured outside.
I looked up at the sky just as the sun began to hide

Now that a new day has just begun.
Whilst the clouds hid the face of the sun
With a cold drink in hand, I made my way under the tree
I stood there for a while as I took in the scenery.

There was a cool breeze that brought comfort from the heat.
For the days have been hot and this breeze was a good treat
Looking out towards the ocean I slowly closed my eyes.
And listened with my heart to nature's joyous cries.

How much more special this moment would be.
If time was able to stand still just for me
How blessed was I to be lost in this place.
How blessed was I for this moment to embrace.

Strength of a Woman

The strength of a woman cannot be measured
Just like her inner beauty that can only be treasured
She brings to this world a whole new life
Nurtures and moulds it through all her strife

When trouble comes knocking at her door
She reaches within for the strength she has in store
With head held high, she charges fearlessly
Or stands firm against any adversity

She is gentle and caring when she needs to be
She is warm and loving for all to see
But never for a minute think that she is weak
For the strength of a woman is what all men seek.

Cherish and love her every day
Cherish and love her come what may
For the strength of a woman is much stronger
When she has support alongside her.

The Greatest Story Ever Told

History has taught us about the greatest story ever told.
It was about a baby boy, born in a stable dark and cold.
The only place was a manger filled with hay.
Where his sweet head, this baby got to lay.

Shepherds, Wisemen and Kings three
Travelled to Bethlehem for a baby to come see.
Carrying gifts of incense, myrrh, and gold
Kings paid homage as the story is told.

25th of December is a day of great joy.
For it is the day that Earth received the heavenly boy
A day that is celebrated by one and all.
Even the earthly creatures great and small

As the day called Christmas slowly comes near
Joyous melodies from the angels we get to hear.
Songs that warm the heart and soul
Songs of Christmas new and old

Enjoying the festivities as we hear Carols being sung.
Cherish the glad tidings as decorations are being hung.
Embrace the joy that we get to share.
May you have a Merry Christmas and a Happy New Year.

February 14th

There is something special coming our way.
A moment in time for your feelings to display.
A day for lovers has been set aside.
Where secret feelings no longer hide.

February 14th is a day to look forward to
A day when lovers prepare special things to do.
To capture the heart of that special person in their life
Some even get to propose to their future wife.

As the day approaches, plans are set in motion,
As many await in great anticipation.
They don't have a clue of what to expect.
For the secrets of the day are always well-kept.

Bonds of love are bound together.
A love that they hope to last forever.
To make time to plan your own special day.
And express your true feelings in everything you say.

Open your heart and set your feelings free.
Ensure your true emotions they get to see.
Love from the heart should never be locked away.
Be bold and make the most of this Valentine's Day.

Valentine's Day

With February fast approaching, there is a buzz in the air
Of lovers finding ways of showing how much they care
With feelings deep within they will go out of their way.
To shower their loved ones with gifts to celebrate
Valentine's Day.

Not everyone gets to express how they feel
For some out there, Valentine's is not a big deal
Some are single and not by choice
Whilst some have lost their inner voice

For some chocolates from a friend would suffice
Or even flowers from a stranger can melt their heart of ice
Though you are single feel free to go out and play
Cause not only lovers get to enjoy Valentine's Day.

You are blessed with life so go make the most
Don't choose to be alone and live like a ghost
Untie your hands and remove that rope
Open your heart to a world filled with hope
Embrace that moment as it comes your way
Enjoy the magic of Valentine's Day.

Thoughts of You

Thoughts of you flood my mind every day
They drive me crazy in every which way
The memories that we shared will forever be treasured
Whilst my feelings for you could never be measured

As time goes by turning days into months and then into years
The void left behind is like walking down never-ending stairs
I wish that I could turn back the hands of time
And relive those precious moments when you were mine

Wishful thinking is all that I have to keep
Even at night, those memories rob me of my sleep
With the amount of time that has passed us by
Those precious moments shared will never die

Thank you for sharing your love with me
And allowing my heart to roam so free
Enjoy the future and what it may bring
I wish you love, joy, and happiness above all things.

THE SHOW MUST GO ON
(Dedicated to Rajiv Mothie)

The show must go on a catchphrase of note.
Used in entertainment for their stories to promote.
The dedication they show when they take to the stage.
Will capture the mind, heart, and soul of every age.

He is a local entertainer with a heart of gold.
Filled with passion and energy to rock your world.
He doesn't ride a horse or pretend to be Prince Valiant
But his performance on stage is nothing but brilliant.

His flair for the arts is nothing less than amazing.
His performance on stage is unequivocally mesmerizing.
He has built a multi-cultural team of locally talented youth.
Fusing South African and Indian dance that is silky and smooth.

Backed by the Big M brand he will take you on a journey.
This amazing individual is none other than Raviv Mothie
If you feel the need to be motivated
Go to his shows and you will never be disappointed.

The Key That Unlocked All Doors
(Dedicated to Salish and Shanice Nandlal)

My heart ran rampant as my eyes met yours
The love in your voice was the key that unlocked all doors.
I knew from the start that I would make you mine
To cherish and love you forever through time.

When you accepted my advances and took me into your heart
I made it my life's mission that nothing will steer us apart.
As years pass us by and our love becomes stronger
My heart remains content as our journey grows longer.

This journey we are on is at our own pace.
A journey that has brought us here to this place.
As we stand together and make this dream come true
I promise to love and cherish you in all that we do.

As I extend my hand to you today
Remember this moment and all that I say.
Take my hand and walk with me.
As husband and wife forever, it shall be

Sorrow

Each morning, I awake I ask myself
What must I do differently to enjoy this life
I start my day with the hope of a better tomorrow
So, I go out positively hiding my sorrow

How long can I continue to ignore this void
How can I go on being ignored
Answers for these questions I fear to ask
Let me embrace this life wearing a mask

I dare not look back at the mistakes I have made
For I know with time they will slowly fade
With hope that the future will help me grow
Even though those mistakes dealt a heavy blow

I choose not to let this sorrow control me
I choose not to let sadness consume me
I will find a way to challenge my sorrow
Allowing for the happiness within to once again flow

SHE IS...
(Girl Empowerment – 7 Hills Primary School)

Her heart was cold, but her eyes were caring.
She is young but her spirit is daring.
She is a child but mature in wisdom.
Using only her words she can command a kingdom.

She is taken for granted and cast aside.
Don't be fooled by the great strength within she chooses to hide!
She does not protest much nor show her true emotions.
Neither does she ask for anyone's opinions.

She is one of a kind, a lady brimming with class.
Her outer beauty is not something one can easily pass.
She is young, strong, and independent.
And with all her achievements she is quite content.

A dynamic individual is what you will find.
If you underestimate her strength, she will leave you behind.
Filled with a zest to live she can take on life on her own.
Fearlessly she will step on you, leaving your heart forlorn.

Don't pity her for she is not weak!
Your approval is not something that she will seek.
She is no Xerox copy if that's what you search for
She is an original like no other you have seen before.

Our Lives

Our lives are not measured by how long we are on earth
Nor of the bad things that we have done since birth
It's not measured by the wisdom that we have achieved.
Nor for the losses that we have grieved

Our lives are not measured by the places we have been
Nor of the countless things that we have seen
It's not measured by the mistakes that we have made
Nor of the memories of our childhood which begin to fade.

It could be measured by the good deeds that we do
Even if people who were impacted never knew
Or by the happiness and joy that we got to spread
For a good name is all that is left behind once you are dead

So, make sure to be kind to others by showing them love
For your life is measured not below but by the man above
Think about your actions and all that you do
So that when you stand for judgment it's not to hell where you go.

LOVE OVER PAIN.

I could only imagine the tears running down her face
I felt the pain in her voice as she slipped from grace
I searched for the right words to ease her mind
But my search was in vain, for no fitting words I could find

Beaten, broken and cast aside
From this world all her pain she chooses to hide
What is it that ties her down to his abuse
Over everything in this world, why is he the one she still will choose

I could only listen to her pain-ridden voice
I shouted in my head" Woman you have a choice."
But the strength of her love was beyond her pain
A woman bearing hardship, beside him she will remain

I asked myself "What had she done wrong."
Tell me Lord how much longer must she trudge along
Then her words came flooding back, reminding me of her love within
And for that love, she chooses there beside him to remain.

Durban Book Fair
(Special thanks to Anivesh &Kiru)

I woke up this morning, head spinning with excitement.
I was going to join a team filled with extraordinary talent.
Authors of note that were filled with stories unending.
Showcasing their books for all that was attending.

I was greeted by the rain as I made my way out my door.
Cool-weather today for a change was definitely in store.
How blessed were we for the mood was already being set.
What perfect weather for a Book Fair from the heavens to get.

We arrived at Simbithi and were amazed at the sight.
Although it was raining the surroundings was truly a delight
The ambiance of this place took our breath away
As we got lost in its beauty wishing longer to stay

The organizers were prompt and started on time.
The special interviewers brought were energetic and sublime.
Their questions and interaction allowed the discussions to flow.
They brought the best out of the Authors who let their emotions go.

I listened attentively as each one got to speak.
Hoping that when my time is near, I will not freak.
I was greeted by S'bo Vilakazi, who was an amazing soul.
Our interaction from the start was on point and under control.

We spoke through the hour like friends of old.
Of the poems that I wrote and the Dreams that were told
What an eventful day it turned out to be
What awesome memories are now stored within me?

Thanks to the organizers of the Durban Book Fair
For showing us authors how much you care
Thanks to all that was present for coming along.
Thanks for giving us the courage to stand up strong.

Beachwood Country Club

The mood was set at the start of the day
And we were ready to get the game underway
The sun smiled down and brightened up the place
Whilst people moved around at their own pace

We were there for a round of golf at Beachwood Country Club
I was in the company of Andy, Ivan, and Suren from Alliance Golf Club
We played our best as we challenged each other
And at the end of the game, we were joined by Suren's sweet Mother

We met at the 19th hole for a round of drinks
Whilst Suren and his mum enjoyed a scrumptious meal
The food was amazing and so was the crowd
There was live music that was not so loud

The ladies serving was intoxicating on their own
When they walked by you could hear the men groan
That was a day of magic without a Magician
The 19th at Beachwood can be a setting for a new tradition.

World Kindness Day

Every beautiful sunrise reminds us of new beginnings.
The ability to reset and abandon our shortcomings.
To embrace the natural beauty that surrounds us all
To embrace humanity big and small

Forget the past and all its disappointments.
Let's journey together in search of new commitments.
Life has taught us that we cannot time-ravel
But together as one, new beginnings we can unravel.

Let's look to the future with hope unending.
Let's support each other with strength unwavering!
Bringing peace, love, and joy to one and all
Supporting each other so that we do not fall
Let's spread the love in all that we do and say
Let's make every day World Kindness Day.

Unending Love

Memories of our first encounter came flooding in
A time when excitement I could not hold within
Your innocent smile captured my heart.
Was it infatuation or love, I could not tell it apart.

I later managed to get you alone at last.
We danced through the night and a spell was cast.
Every moment since then was a dream come true.
In me was born an unending love for you

From teenagers to adults, we marched along.
Mistakes were made but our love stood strong.
As we stand here together facing another day
Here's me wishing you a Happy Anniversary.

This Christmas

Many years have come and gone
When a baby boy to this world was born
Wrapped in swaddling clothes, lying in a manger.
This child was sent down to earth to be our saviour.

His birth to all, a special gift
As he was sent from heaven for our spirits to lift
His mission is to bring joy to the world and save all mankind.
He raised the dead, healed the sick and even gave sight to the blind.

The world is a buzz as Christmas draws near.
Excitement and celebrations now fill up the air.
Breaking out in carols from Jingle Bells to Silent Night
Remembering the star that shone ever so bright.

Let's come together in a joyous celebration.
Spreading love to all on this festive occasion
Let's make this Christmas a day of pleasure.
And let Christ This Christmas be in our hearts forever.

Restless

It rained quite heavy throughout the night
I was restless and with my bedding, I picked a fight
Tossing and turning in search of some sleep
I tried for hours, I even tried counting sheep

I needed my beauty sleep I heard myself say
As I would struggle to take on the coming day
Two hours have passed, and I am still awake
I am hoping to fall asleep before daybreak.

I was losing this battle to put my mind at ease
What can I do can someone help me, please
My thoughts are flowing when it should be at rest
Come tomorrow I won't be at my best

I closed my eyes and tried hard not to think
Hoping that in a deep sleep, I will eventually sink
Sometimes as the night slowly dwindled away
I eventually fell asleep hip hip hooray.

Infectious Smile

I know that my heart was tricked that day
When this beauty I met took my breath away
Her infectious smile lured me to that place
Whilst instantaneously bringing a smile to my face

In all that haze I had forgotten why I was there
Whilst in a trance-like state all I could do was stare
As I saw her walking straight towards me
I turned my eyes away so that I could break free

Her melodious voice jolted me to my feet
How can I help you sir as our eyes came to meet
My heart was racing like a speedboat
My mind praying that my voice won't get stuck in my throat

Yes, you may, that was my spontaneous reaction.
Tell me please if those shoes are your latest edition
In one smooth motion, she turned to where I was pointing
Yes, they are, was her reply without even hesitating

Trying to stay calm I started to speak in a low tone
Then I was saved by the ringing of my phone
I excused myself and walked out the door
I knew she was only eye candy as I walked away from the store.

In You

In you, I found a new hope to stand up tall
To face all adversities even should I fall
In you, I have found a reason to embrace the dark
To release all doubt and to make my mark.

In you, I found a love unwavering
To fill my life with happiness unending.
In you, I found that special one
That brings warmth to my life like the summer sun

In you, I found the will to live
A life where joy to all I can freely give
In you, I found that ray of hope
That will guide me through the slipperiest of slope

In you, I have learned that love has no boundaries
And that life can have more tranquillity than worries
In you my Lord I will forever be grateful.
Giving me this talent to make others' lives more meaningful.

Her...

Her skin was soft and creamy.
Her eyes were wide and dreamy.
Her voice was soft and gentle.
And the music she listened to was nothing but sentimental.

Her beauty was mesmerising.
Her body was oh so tantalising.
Her graceful walk would put you into a trance.
And she can capture your heart with just one glance.

I tried to walk up to her and pour out my heart!
But my legs won't move as I watched her depart.
Should I stop her before she goes out of sight?
But my voice got lost as my braveness took flight.

All chances were lost as I watched her walk away.
Now my heart is troubled as my feelings I failed to say.
Hopefully, with time, I could build up some courage.
Until we meet again, I can only treasure her parting image.

Fear of Rejection

Nervous, shy, and afraid of rejection
Locked in my heart I hide my intentions.
I watch her from afar, lost in a dream-like state.
Wondering what life would be like if I was her mate.

Time passed by, and I kept my distance.
Overcoming rejection was my greatest resistance
As maturity set in, I hoped our paths would cross.
So, I can stand up strong and make up for my loss

When that time did come, I was not able to shake off my fear
So, away from her path I chose to stay clear
No matter how confident I thought I felt
With this fear of rejection, my strength did melt.

Silently I sink into a bottomless pit
When alone with my feelings I choose to sit
Hoping that with time my feelings won't wither.
and my fear will allow us to be together.

New Year

Just as the dust settles on another Christmas past
We look towards the New Year that's closing in fast
As realisation hits home of time passing by
We can only ponder on our losses and sigh

We look back at our achievements throughout the year
Cherished memories we choose to hold dear
Whilst new dreams run through our mind
We hope for a better New Year to find

I drown out all negativity of failed aspirations
I weed out all my problems and constraints
I choose to drown out all my sorrow
I choose to be the change for a better tomorrow.

A Milestone

Today marks a special occasion
Where you will receive an overload of affection
Loved ones will make this day shine bright
Celebrations will continue until late in the night

I pray for love and joy in abundance
May you get to cherish this moment, sing and dance
A milestone has been reached by you
I pray that all your wishes come true

Here's wishing you a happy birthday
May God's grace be with you as you celebrate this day
Have an amazing birthday my dear friend
May you enjoy these words to you I send.

The Promise

We were both young when our paths first collided
A promise of a vow one day to be carried.
From the moment I laid eyes on you nothing else mattered
Love took over, whilst my loneliness scattered

As time trudged along, new memories were created
And as our lives entwined a promise was stated
That one day in the future our lives will be defined
Where together as one our journey will be aligned

As we celebrate our anniversary today
Thank you for the memories my heart gets to display
The joys of that promise have not steered us wrong
May they forever on our journey and remain strong.

The Language of Flowers

Deeper meanings lie within the language of flowers.
Take roses for example, with their variation of colours.
Red roses are for true love, whilst blue is for mystery.
Black roses are for death whilst white signifies innocence and purity.

Yellow roses are for friendship whilst orange is for passion.
But the warmth that it gives to the recipient is the greatest satisfaction.
Then there are the tulips which symbolises a perfect and deep love
Mother nature's gift is given to us from the heavens above.

Then we see the Sunflower that is bright, cheery, and warm.
Known as happy flowers it can make you mellow and calm.
The flower that can replace the rose is the carnation.
For they symbolise devotion, love, and a deep fascination.

No matter the occasion that may come your way.
There is a flower out there that will brighten any day.
For the world is filled with flowers of majestic beauty.
That brings can bring to life an ambience of serenity.

Sugar and Spice

Women are made of sugar and spice.
With an extra topping of all things nice
She can sometimes be sweet and gentle.
And there are times of moody and temperamental.

She can smother you with her loving arms.
And blow your mind away with her simplistic charms.
She can brave the mightiest of storms to be by your side.
Exposing her true feelings which she chooses not to hide.

So, cherish every moment together, through time.
Love her unconditionally, for it isn't any crime.
Hold her in your arms and show her how much you care.
Reassure her, that no matter what you will always be there.
A shoulder to lean on should she so desire
A pillar of strength, should she ever tire.

Scars

The journey of life has many twists and turns.
Some penetrate the heart and forever burn.
Memory and scars are all that are left behind.
Some are visible whilst some are hard to find.

To the bearer of these scars, the journey is rough.
Fighting this pain daily is always tough.
They soldier along as they hide this pain.
No matter their strength, they eventually take the strain.

Visual scars are there to show that you have healed.
Embrace beautiful memories shared, so that all pain is sealed.
Use these scars to make a brand-new start.
Cherish those moments and free your heart.
Your journey may be tough by the scars we don't see.
Allow your heart from this pain, to somehow be free.

Precious Cargo

The ship has sailed, but precious cargo lost.
The journey ahead now comes at a high cost.
Emotionally battered and bruised.
A heart shattered; a mind left confused.

How could I have taken things for granted?
My life is now hollow, my emotions left haunted.
A high price was paid for letting you go.
The reality of it all is a tremendous blow.

Should I hide my pain, or should I change my style?
Or hide all my troubles behind a smile.
Should I renew my search for my precious cargo?
Or should I weather the storm and sail to Key Largo?
I believe that some things are best set free.
If it comes back, then it was meant to be.

Hearts Cries

Tears from this heart's cries have finally subsided.
Realisation has set in, that your love has departed.
With time I pray these wounds will heal
But never will I forget that this pain was real.

Head bowed down I will gather my thoughts.
It was self-inflicted, this pain that has left me in knots.
I will not allow myself to be drowned in sorrow.
But embrace life, and work towards a better tomorrow.

For the love that we shared was deep and pure
And for this love, this pain I will endure.
Time may heal all wounds, but your memories forever will remain.
Whilst I allow my inner strength to take care of this pain

I choose not to let this pain consume me.
I know that one day my heart will be free.
Free to allow for a new love to blossom.
A love that will release me from this pain-filled ransom.

Fictitious Smile

Curiosity got the better of me as I watched him pass by
His facial expression is what first caught my eye
There was a big smile painted across his face
But to me, that smile looked out of place

I watched as he started to look around
His lips were moving but I heard no sound
I walked up to him, curious as hell
What's with this fictitious smile, please do tell

Caught off guard he said, "What do you mean".
Judging by your expression there is something that you have seen.
I see you smiling but not out of joy
You look like a kid who lost his favourite toy.

His response was amazing and somewhat grand
Why be sympathetic to the situation at hand
Wearing a fictitious smile keeps my worries at bay
It gives me hope to brighten up my day.

I smiled to myself for I just got schooled.
A fictitious smile can get your worries fooled.
A priceless gesture to chase your troubles away
With me, this fictitious smile forever will stay.

Emotional Maze

I am lost in this emotional maze.
Head spinning, I walk around in a daze.
Searching frantically for a way out
Trusting my inner voice, I shrugged off all doubt.

This journey I choose will leave me weary.
The days ahead I will prevent from becoming dreary.
I trust that I will ride these waters rough.
With confidence that I can handle any stuff

I don't consider this a failure or a sign of defeat.
For my battles not lost whilst I am still on my feet
I know that I will find my way out of this emotional maze.
And I will treat this only as a passing phase.

A Troubled Mind

A troubled mind lost amongst a million stars
A broken heart bearing unhealing scars
Treasured memories fill a heart of stone
Of a youthful soul that is left to fend on her own

Tears are the only comfort for her troubled mind
In search of happiness hoping one day to find
Which will help break her stone-cold heart
Where her miseries from within will eventually depart

Her cry out for help brings her new hope
Reassuring herself, that she is not at the end of her rope
With a positive mindset, she will find great strength
And ride the wave till her heart is content

A Good-Hearted Woman
(A Tribute to Pinky Mothie)

A good-hearted woman is what we get to see
She embodies an angel robed in humanity
Her passion to unleash hidden gems upon us all
Being a mother of Culture is her earthly call

She acknowledges the women who fight for a worthy cause
With the Big M brand, she dares not to pause
With passion unwavering she created Influential Women
In honour of their fights, she ignores creed, colour, or religion

Her kids are not the only ones brimming with pride
She welcomes everyone wanting to be by her side
I thank the heavens for sharing this angel with us all
I'm thankful to have the opportunity to see inside her crystal ball.

Oh, mother of Culture may your journey be forever blessed
You are to us more precious than a crowns beautiful crest

Three Words

With just three words a heart you can steal
To that special someone, these words are surreal.
Words which they thought, they wouldn't hear.
Words from the heart, which the future makes clear.

How incredibly special these words could be.
Especially when they set one's emotions free.
Free to attract hope, tranquillity and joy.
Free for a new life upon this world to deploy.

How powerful are these words, when spoken from the heart
For it unleashes new hope for a fresh, bright start.
A start that will help the love within to flourish.
These words are inner happiness, for all to unleash.

These three words bring harmony to life.
Can cut away through sorrow like a hot knife.
These three magical words that our hearts choose to say.
Will bring new hope ito your life every day.

The Journey to Now

We were young, energised teenagers.
With a goal not to be failures
In search of adventure and knowledge
We realised that not all were destined for college.

With a great sense of appreciation.
A special bond became God's creation.
We were brought together in friendship.
Which later fused into a magical relationship.

With an amazing desire, we connected with one another.
This special bond has stood firm like no other.
We have graciously matured through time.
While some still remained partners in crime.

Our friendship stood firm; our hearts remained strong.
In this amazing group is where our love belongs.
Our lives and journeys have brought us together.
Let's cherish this opportunity forever.

No Disguise

Tears streaming down from her eyes.
She let it all out, she wore no disguise.
The pain was etched across her beautiful face.
I was tempted to walk across and give her a warm embrace.
She did not care who saw her cry.
For she paid no heed to those passing her by
I quietly walked up and sat beside her.
At her tears-stained face, I could only stare.

I held all emotions when she looked at me.
I'm here for support so set your feelings free.
I took her in my arms and whispered in her ear.
Don't hold back your tears as I drew her near.

The best way to deal with the pain within
Is to let it all out, so that you can breathe freely again.
Thank you, my friend, for the words of encouragement.
Thank you for the shoulder and for sharing your sentiments.

It is good to know that at my lowest I am not alone.
Thank you for planting seeds of joy in my heart of stone.
I will cherish this moment and the warmth that you gave.
I promise that to this sadness I will never be a slave.

Night's Sky

Lighting up a cloudless night is a Galaxy of twinkling stars.
As I gaze up into space, I wonder which one could be Mars.
I heard that men are from Mars and women are from Venus.
A silly thought, for I know that's definitely preposterous.

Sharing the night's sky is a full moon shining ever so bright.
Giving the earth an enchanting look, creating an amazing sight.
As I stood in awe looking at this amazing night's sky.
Taking in these celestial objects that is teasing my mind's eye.

These amazing views that people on earth enjoy for free.
Even the beautiful effects created, where the sky meets the sea.
Phenomenal treasures uncontrolled by time.
Phenomenal treasures that does not cost a dime.

So, take every opportunity to enjoy this sight.
Not only when the night's sky is lit up so bright.
Whilst the stars and the moon dance through the night
Their radian beams is our nights light.

Journey of Life

The journey of life has many twists and turns.
Some penetrate the heart and forever burn.
Memories and scars are all that are left behind.
Some are visible, whilst others are hard to find.

To the bearer of the latter, the journey is rough.
Fighting this pain daily is somewhat tough.
They tend to soldier on hiding their pain.
No matter their strength they eventually take strain.

Visual scars are there to show that the wound has healed.
Embrace the beautiful memories shared, so that all pain is sealed.
Turn these scars into a badge of honour to make a new start.
Cherished memories will help to free your heart.

Your journey through life lies in your own hands.
Take control of your journey and all of life's demands.
You may stumble, and you may fall.
No matter your struggles pick yourself up and stand up tall.

Father

He set me straight, he made me strong.
Watching over me, correcting me when I did wrong.
He held my hand when I lost my way.
He gave me the wisdom not to stray.

My special knight without any armor.
I will cherish every moment we spent together.
Thank you for lifting my spirits when I was sad.
I am truly proud to call you Dad.

Chosen by God to be my father, not just by birth.
You have become my guiding angel here on earth.
Thank you, Daddy, for all you did for me.
Thank you for the life that you have given me, so happy and carefree.

I wish you an abundance of blessings this Father's Day.
May your heart overflow with the love I'm sending your way.
May God continue to keep you in his care.
Be it on Earth or Heaven up there.

Fashion Euphoria

A fashion Euphoria integrated with entertainment.
Brought together by the Hands-On Foundation.
With the aim to change people's mindset.
Adding positive thinking and living without any sweat.

Poverty, literacy and mental wellness are some of the projects
on their list.
Empowering the unemployed with tertiary education, ever
willing to assist.
Special training from educators is somewhat lacking.
For facilities and equipment businesses they are attracting.

The amazing Zeeni M, the captain of this ship,
With her crazy sense of humour, she will take you on a wild trip.
On board are special entertainers that you will get to see.
One of those is the phenomenal Rajiv Mothie.

Sibaya Amphitheatre is the place where dreams come true.
A place where Afro Fusion will unleash the excitement within you.
Open your hearts and join hands to support these awesome women.
As they journey together building a stronger united Nation.

A Petite Woman

A petite woman in a male-dominated field.
Nothing deters her and nothing makes her yield.
With manicured fingernails, she grabbed her tool
Jumped into the machine, dang she looked cool.

I was amazed at her action, what a pleasure to watch.
Hoping for her attention, I would somehow catch.
Though the challenge before her seemed to be tough
She gladly embraced it, without a fuss.

Our eyes locked as she turned towards me.
On her face was painted a beautiful smile for all to see.
She caught me off guard rendering me silent for a while.
Releasing some tension, I asked if I could bottle her smile.

Her response was as calm as a summer breeze.
I will take that into consideration, she said with ease.
I left her with that thought, as I walked away.
A perfect icebreaker for when she next comes my way.

Mum

My special person filled with love unwavering.
You stood by me with strength unending.
From the moment that we first met; I melted your heart.
I captured all of you, right from the very start.

Brimming with pride you held on to this child.
Knowing full well that one day, you will be released into the wild
To me, you were the brightest star that lights up my way
Lovingly guiding and watching over me, every day

I am blessed to be your child, the apple of your eyes.
You were wise enough to see through all my lies.
My love for you within my heart is beyond any measure.
Cause to me Mum, you are my greatest treasure.

I thank the Lord for sharing this amazing woman with me.
I will hold you up for the rest of the world to see.
These words from my heart to you I will say.
May you have a blessed and amazing, Mother's Day.

A Forever Moment
(This poem is dedicated to my extended children)

A group of strangers brought together by faith.
A brotherhood formed in a world plagued with hate.
A strong foundation was set, as their lives entwined.
As their journey progressed, their lives were redefined.

Some brothers were lost along the way
Their memories in our hearts forever will stay
No matter the time that passes us by
Only tears of joy, our eyes shall cry.

A forever moment now etched in time.
Whilst their lives have aged, like a fine wine.
From singles to couples some lives have been blessed.
No matter life's challenges, as a team they addressed them.

This evolution unfolded in front of my eyes.
So, the strength of this bond, for me, sheds no surprise.
Families have grown when this brotherhood took form.
May they be forever blessed, as their lives transform.

Youthful Innocence

She was full of excitement as she skipped around
Even stopping to play with little kids in the playground
Her voice echoed as she laughed out loud
Not even stopping as she ran through the crowd

My eyes followed her, as she joyfully went on her way
I was intrigued by her youthfulness and innocent display.
Nothing mattered more than behaving like a child
Whilst holding their hands, being childlike and wild.

If only the adults of this world can see what I saw
This youthful innocence could open any door
Leading us all into a magical place
Where evil and destruction hold no base

This amazing memory I will treasure through time
Encased in youthful innocence, creating a new paradigm
Let us not forget the innocence of our youth
Living those moments we will appreciate divine truth.

Thank You Daddy

I learned that I brought you to tears when we first met.
I changed your life, and you had no regret
I was the positive outlook as your new journey began
Filled with new responsibilities you hatched out a plan.
As time passed by, you left me wanting for naught.
Self-confidence was gained as I learned a lot
You never spared the rod when I was wrong.
You showed me how to be brave, you made me strong.

The values you instilled have shaped my mind
Giving me the wisdom to always be kind
I appreciate all that you had to do
Nothing comes close to the love I hold for you

Thank you, Daddy, for being there for me
Thank you for opening my eyes for the world to see
I will hold your teachings as a beacon of light
And by those teachings, I promise to always do right.

As I now face the world as a father of my very own
I will instill in my kids your teachings, as I have grown
Moulding their lives I will be brimming with pride
Thank you, Dad, for always being there by my side.

Sweet Yet Sassy

Sweet yet sassy, our Angel divine
Innocence personified, this daughter of mine
Making us proud in all that she sets out to do
Radiant being, may all your dreams come true
A milestone reached, as we hand you the key
Nothing but the love we bestow upon thee.

May your birth be etched forever in time.
May the years ahead be nothing but sublime.
Embrace your youth as you continue your journey.
Thank the heavens every day, as you write your own story.
Be true to yourself and never back down.
Stand up strong, keeping your feet firm on the ground.

Lead Her Ship

She chose her career, without any fear
In a male-dominated arena, her path was not clear.
Driven by passion to excel in her field
Nothing deters her, nor makes her yield.

Every day brings a new challenge her way
Yet from this path, she dares not stray.
She approaches life with a positive mindset.
Leaving her troubles behind, she hits reset.

With a vision to one day Lead Her Ship.
I applaud her tenacity in taking a firm grip.
She encourages her Teammates to soldier on.
Gaining respect from everyone.

She has a built-in ability to multi-task.
And when help is needed, she is not afraid to ask.
Without any fear, she leads from the front.
Without hesitation, she will shoulder the brunt.

Her Leadership qualities have not gone unseen
If you show, that for growth, you are willing and keen.
It's here for you, to take and embrace,
The support that is needed to grow in this place

Earth Angels

Earth Angels sent here to be amongst us all.
Fulfilling the Lord's work, heeding his call.
Spreading his word and renewing the faith.
Creating for God's people, a tranquil state.

Chosen as missionaries on this journey long.
Filled with the Holy Spirit to keep them strong.
They follow his path, as they soldier on.
Filled with strength from the Father, Spirit and Son.

We are blessed with Earth Angels here in our town.
Bringing a message from our King who wore thorns for a crown.
Thank you for lifting our Spirits and enriching our minds.

Thank you for opening our hearts eyes that were blind.
As their journey in our hometown comes to an end
Our prayers and love, with these earth angles we send.
May your journey be filled with strength in abundance
To continue your mission, brimming with confidence.

Diversity and Inclusion

We live in a country dubbed the Rainbow Nation
So, we stride ahead leaving nothing to misinterpretation.
In our places of work, we have an infusion of cultures.
Which through time, will prove our greatest of treasures

Diversity allows for lateral thinking.
Fussing different ideologies, a network that's linking.
Teams working together share different perspectives.
Striving in unison towards one desired objective.

Diversity and inclusion are aimed at one and all.
Injecting passion in learning for leadership to stand tall.
Lateral thinkers often embrace new change.
Allowing for growth, whilst some just rearrange.

A brilliant concept for strengthening the team
Releasing future leaders to pursue their dreams.
May all this planning and hard work come to fruition.
As together we continue to strive to become one strong Nation.

Cherished......

From mountains high to valleys low
From barren lands to watching flowers grow
From rivers wide, to oceans deep
Cherished adventures I will forever keep

From Amazing Grace to Our Father
From the Book of Genesis to the Holy Order
From keeping the faith to heavenly blessings
My cherished passions unto him I'm entrusting.

From Snow White to Ella
From Red Riding Hood to Cinderella
From a journey of deceit to a love unending
Cherished stories will always remain everlasting
.
From finding true love and letting go of pain
From holding back tears to dancing in the rain
From Endless Love to Stuck on You
I will cherish every memory of a love so true.

Can I .....

Can I walk with you down this lonely path
And allow me to fix your broken heart.
Can I hold your hand as we slowly walk
Even if you choose not to talk.

Can I sit beside you by the firelight
And just enjoy the tranquillity of the night.
Can I put my hand around your shoulder
as the night's air starts to get colder?

Can I show you how precious you really are
How one day to someone you can be a special star
Can I tell you that with time, you will find new love
It's written in the heavens above.

Can I ask you to put your pain aside
And take new possibilities in your stride
I can honestly tell you all this, my friend
You have the answers within, for your broken heart to mend.

Amazing Dancer
(Fiona Pillay)

Fuelled with endless energy to dance
With her graceful moves, she will put you in a trance.
Sweet, confident and sporting an elegant demeanour
She will, without a doubt, make you quiver.

She effortlessly commands the stage
Keeping those watching, fully engaged.
She encourages the other dancers to give their best
Even surpassing her limits, with no thought of rest.

I was captivated by what I got to see
This amazing dancer, entertaining me.
Like the rest of the audience, I was truly amazed.
As she continued with her dance leaving us all dazed.

The performance, unfortunately, had to end.
Our best wishes and love to her were all we could send.
I pray, that her passion for the arts, never strays.
May she be abundantly filled with heavenly blessings every day.

A Beautiful Heart

Encased inside a beautiful heart is a story untold.
Of an amazing woman in need of warmth from the cold.
She longs to be held in a loving embrace
This is something that can bring a smile to her face.

The time has come for her to break out of her comfort zone.
With the hope that she will not be forever alone.
Knowing that the future may not be what it seems
In pursuit of happiness, she chases after her dreams.

She put her head down not to catch his gaze
Scared of the thought of setting her heart ablaze
As realisation sets in, she starts to waver
For she has been patiently waiting for her true love to save her.

The Boys from Alliance

A beautiful morning was greeted by the sounds of the sea.
The sun's rays filtered through the clouds, smiling down on me.
Lost in thought as I sat listening to the waves crashing.
Basking in the sunlight, whilst watching the water splashing.

I caught the sounds of friends' voices, echoing in the background.
As they took turns teasing one another and forging a new bond.
The boys from Alliance on a golfing weekend down the coast.
And as the spirits flowed, each one decided to make a toast.

Great respect was shown, between the young and the old.
Whilst they merrily sipped on their drinks, enjoying it cold.
The morale in the camp was amazing to see.
More rewarding than the serenity of the sea.

A weekend of golfing, one filled with pleasure.
A weekend which we all will truly treasure.
Though the winds were strong making golfing tough.
The time spent bonding was undoubtedly the right stuff.

Stories

Chasing dragons, chasing myths
Chasing stories with gory bits
Life as a writer holds no boundaries.
Every adventure they fashion into stories.

Trick or treat or guns and roses.
Including fashion models and all their poses,
Cannot hide from the might of the pen.
As they make up stories of now and then.

Musicians, actors, casts and crew,
They weed them all out, slyly they do.
Showing no fear of going out on a limb.
In search of stories from the cold to the grim.

From a saucy tale to words that rhyme.
Authors and poets, make the most of their time.
Penning their word for the entire world to see
Even sharing stories with you and me.

My Heart will be Thine

I will shout out my feelings for the world to know.
Should it be from a mountain or valleys below?
When you hear my heart's cry, give me a sign.
And know that forever my heart will be thine.

Though the road ahead looks somewhat bleak
I put trust in our love that it will never grow weak.
I will merge into the shadows leaving my heart to pine.
Knowing that forever my heart will be thine.

My head is spinning, my world is upside down.
My heart is submerged in tears, and it's starting to drown.
I pray for strength whilst I search for a lifeline.
Knowing full well that forever my heart will be thine.

I search for positive thoughts which I will hold very dear.
Losing your love is my greatest fear.
I will live with the hope that one day our lives will entwine.
Never forget that forever my heart will be thine

My African Queen

My African queen, a woman of beauty,
A goddess of love, looking somewhat sultry.
She captured my attention without any effort.
My mind was left in a mess as I started to flirt.

As I sit here enjoying this amazing view.
Inwardly hoping to spend time with you.
My heart is racing, and my mind in a trance.
Tell me please, do I stand a chance?

I cannot take my gaze away from your sexy booty.
Your body is intoxicating, I tell you truly.
As I stand to take my leave and say goodbye.
I hope to receive a favourable reply.

An African queen is what you truly are.
A seductive temptress, behind the bar.
I wish I could take you in my arms.
And woe you endlessly with all my charms.

Music Man

Play us a song Mr music Man, Play us a beautiful song.
Help free our minds, so we can joyfully sing along.
Play us a song filled with love and laughter.
Let us live in the moment and not dwell in the ever after.

Play us a song that makes our body move to the beat.
As the darkness closes in, may it also move our feet.
Play us a song that teases our minds and soul.
Make every beat want to make us lose control.

Play us a magical song, Mr Music Man.
Fill us with unlimited passion as only you can.
Play us a song that speaks volumes in our minds.
May it unleash the happiness within that only you could find.

So, play us a song Mr Music man, play us a beautiful song.
Give courage to the weak so that can dance the whole night long.
Play us a song that will take our breath away.

From Author to Publisher

A qualified doctor, with a brilliant mind
With a passion for writing, she left medicine behind.
From author to publisher, she embraced the change.
Never looking back, she took on the challenge.

She shrugged off all fear, of starting anew.
Whilst strategically assembling a dynamic crew.
With grit and determination, she managed her team.
While never giving up, chasing after her dream.

The fruits of her labour, a CEO she has become.
All the while giving seasoned publishing houses a run.
Accolades are flowing quickly and fast,
As this young lady moves forward with a dynamic blast.

A soft-spoken lady with a heart of gold.
She takes care of her authors both young and old.
Keli Hariparsad is her name.
And Publishing books is her primary game.

Heavenly Blessings

The sun was hidden as a new day started.
I'm hoping that positive thoughts were planted.
Lost in the moment, I stood enjoying this sight.
Taking in heavenly blessings as my spirits ignite.

Looking at this cloud-filled sky that greeted us all.
Listening to the pitter patter as raindrops began to fall.
I was captivated by how calm the world felt.
In your embrace, all negative thoughts began to melt.

The air was fresh, cool and filled with wetness.
The ambiance created was nothing short of greatness.
I'm ever so thankful for Mother Nature.
For bringing such tranquillity, like a perfect treasure.

Many have lost sight of this amazing feeling.
Amidst the daily struggles that they are facing.
Take a moment and embrace nature at its best.
Allow yourself to let go, relax and take a rest.

Counting Stars

One, two, three, four, five, six, seven
Counting stars that's looking down from heaven.
Scattered across the sky like tiny lights.
Whilst shooting stars are nothing but meteorites

A blessing to earth is these wonders we see.
Like the stars on high, I wish I was able to roam free.
To merrily dance among the stars and moon.
In a trance-like state to a heavenly tune.

The closest of the solar elements is the moon.
Floating amongst the stars like a balloon.
It changes shapes through phases and time.
Whilst among the stars they do look sublime

One, two, three, four, five, six, seven
Counting stars for children was somewhat a given.
Watching them light up the nights sky.
Are these twinkling lights that catches our eye.

A Seasoned Pro

Reminiscent of a scene from a Bollywood movie
As she stepped out the door looking somewhat groovy.
I was transfixed by her sultry gait.
Neven if time stopped, I was prepared to wait.

I followed her movement whilst her long hair hung free.
I was hypnotised by this angel walking gracefully towards me.
I watched as the wind gently blew her hair.
I gathered my thoughts when I heard her say, "Hi there".

A smile danced on my face, trying not to look like a fool.
Hi, I must say that you look kinder cool.
We drove off together away from her place.
All through the journey, I threw glances at her beautiful face.

We chatted with ease as we continued on our way.
I learned a lot about her on that magical day.
I admired the way she carried herself through it all.
Nothing could deter nor make her fall.

Her youthful innocence was hidden from sight.
Even her earlier fear had suddenly taken flight.
She went through the questions like a seasoned pro.
If she had any fear, nobody would know.

A Beacon of Light

To me, she is as sweet as a piece of candy.
And as warm as a sip of brandy
She can be as quiet as a church mouse.
And as devastating as a burning house

She can wrap me around her little finger.
Giving me the chills like it's the middle of winter.
She can leave me lost in her smouldering eyes.
And like a Gypsy, taking with her my heart's cries.

She is a beacon of light when life is dark.
And as straight as an arrow never missing her mark.
I hope she loves me forever as I give her my all.
When times are tough, may she heed my call.

As together as a family we celebrate your special day.
Remember that we love you unconditionally come what may.
We salute you; we adore you and most of all we appreciate you.
From us all may all your birthday wishes come true.

Happy birthday my wife ukhule nenhlonipho sthandwasami nokumazi omunye mutu, aphinde nkulunkulu asiphe eminye iminyaka sindawonye

Treacherous Heat

The sky was naked no clouds were in sight.
The sun was relentless shining ever so bright.
We looked for shade at every chance we got.
The sun's rays were torturous and scary hot.

The wind was welcoming from this treacherous heat.
But amongst the trees, we found no seat.
We stood for a while under its shade.
Which was not for long as it started to fade.

Back under the sun, we found ourselves standing.
Like herded cattle awaiting branding.
I felt the sun's rays burn into my skin.
I felt droplets of sweat run down my shin.

I was starting to turn purple I jokingly said.
Away from this heat, I was finally led.
When I stopped, I found myself inside a bar.
Turning to my friend I said, you are truly a superstar.

The beer was cold, and it was a welcome feeling.
This ice-cold liquid gave me the pleasure of just chilling.
The rest of the day was spent kicking back.
It was a lot better than letting my skin turn black.

SUNFLOWER

The beauty of the Sunrise reminds us of a precious gift.
To appreciate all our loved ones and their spirits too.
As we breathe in this new day filled with endless possibilities.
Let's do what we can, as we explore all opportunities.

Filled with a passion and desire to make a positive start.
Let's embrace the sunlight as it warms our cold heart.
Like a sunflower standing proud as it absorbs the sun's rays.
With a resounding strength, smiling through the hottest of days.

This amazing flower that's yellow and gold,
Represents a friendship that lasts forever, I'm told.
Emitting positive energy and good vibes is the sunflower.
Filling hearts with happiness all through the summer.
If you ever receive a sunflower, hold it dear.
The strength of a bond, this message rings clear.

Oh, Holy Night

Oh, holy night, when the stars shine ever so bright,
Over a baby boy lying in a manger destined to be our guiding light.
His presence on earth, through an immaculate conception.
To walk amongst men and be a living salvation.

A blessing to the world bringing nothing but joy.
The world is still amazed by this baby boy.
Blessed with the miracles that he performed.
Even his teachings still leave many reformed

With the greatest of joys, we celebrate each year.
The story of the birth, of our mighty saviour.
Now December has finally come our way.
Let's spread only love and joy on Christmas Day.

My Love

Around the world, across the seas.
In search of true love, I sail with the breeze.
For my heart is empty and my nights are cold.
I will search the earth until I have my love to hold.

No matter the time, no matter the distance.
Not even challenges can affect my patience.
I will travel the skies; I will travel the lands.
I will only rest when I have my love in my hands.

I know in my heart that my true love is out there.
Someone special, with whom my life I can share.
If through it all, my strength grows weak.
I will never lose hope, in the love that I seek.

Be it day or be it night.
The love that I seek, in my heart shines bright.
When the time is right, and our paths do cross.
This love in my heart forever I will emboss.

Lady In Pink

Her eyes were as blue as a cloudless sky,
Her skin was as white as snow.
She caught me staring, but smiled and winked her eye,
I was taken by surprise, but I went with the flow.

I called over the waiter who served her a drink,
Can you tell me my brother, what's the lady's poison?
Are you referring to the lady in pink?
Yes, it is for her beauty has me somewhat smitten.

When her glass is empty, her next round is on me,
You may point in my direction if she dares to ask.
And I will gladly acknowledge or let her be,
I am curious to see if her smile was not hidden behind a mask.

When her glass was empty, he took over her drink,
He whispered to her as he pointed my way.
She lifted her glass this beautiful lady in pink,
With a big bright smile, she sent kisses my way,

She invited me to her table, where we spoke for a while,
I sat there beside her, praying the night would not end.
I reassured her that flirting was not my style,
But I was glad that I did, for in her I found a new friend.

Games We Played

Skipping stones whilst playing on the riverbank.
Launching paper boats and watching until they sank.
With scuffed up knees we chased after the ball.
Most games we played until our parents would call.

Our summers were worse as the days were long.
We ran through the bushes like warriors strong.
Bows and arrows and slings were weapons we used.
Running around barefoot not fearing to get bruised.

As evening sets in, the games would start to change.
No one was eager to leave, a sight that was never strange.
A poor community filled with kids brimming with pride.
Running around joyfully, with nothing to hide

How times have changed for these games no longer exist.
As the kids of today, for a computer, they dare not resist.
Days of the old is surely no mystery.
If only they could have seen a part of our history.

Dry Ground

I ventured outside as the rain started to gently fall.
Within minutes my gutters were raging like a waterfall.
This gentle rain transformed into an ugly thunderstorm.
Whilst along the roadside a mini river took form.

Protected by the awning I stood on dry ground.
Looking sheepishly out at the water slapping all around.
In the days of my youth, I would embrace the chance.
To run out into the rain and merrily dance.

As time slips away and our inner childhood is lost.
Adulthood takes over, whilst sanity prevails at all costs.
Those years are behind for the world not the same.
Staying safe and healthy is no childish game.

I could only but smile at my lack of spontaneity.
Out of my dream-like state and back to reality
I stood there for a while enjoying the coolness of the rain.
Allowing the invisible water, to wash away my heart's pain.

Dreams

A best-laid plan may never see the light of day.
Would you give up or go in search of another way?
Dreams are the same when you stumble and fall.
A strong mind and perseverance will overcome it all.

For no road out there bares straight paths.
So, prepare for obstacles, before your journey starts.
Be not afraid of what you may find.
Trust in yourself and leave all fears behind.

Be true to your dreams and believe in yourself.
Stow away all doubt at the back of your shelf.
Only a positive mindset will lead you forth.
And truly allow for you to unlock all of your worth.

When the path is in darkness, and you lose all sight.
Search within you for that guiding light.
Follow that dream, wherever you are.
And one day you will shine like the brightest star.

Colour Matters Not

Be it Black, brown, yellow, or white.
Colour matters not if the heart is right.
A sincere sharing of true emotions.
In itself is the strongest of potions.

True feelings will surpass the hardest of tests.
For in each other true love forever rests.
Your journey in life is defined by the seeds you sow.
If you love and nurture it, with strength it will grow.

A selfish decision you choose to make.
Will remain with you, with every step you take.
Fear not if others don't share your views.
Let love be the reason, the path you choose.

When days are dark, and friends are few.
You can turn to the one that stands by you.
Hold them in your arms and keep them near.
The love that is shared is priceless and dear.

Broken Promises

Standing in front of a mirror is a figure filled with sadness.
Looking back was a face lost in total darkness.
A broken, tormented soul in search of happiness.
With a moral so low she would grasp at emptiness.

How could the one she trusted render her helpless?
Turning her life upside down filled with nothingness.
How to encourage her that her life is priceless?
And give her the strength to overcome broken promises.

Show her that life is better without his abusiveness.
Whilst being appreciated again is nothing short of effortless.
Love and joy in the world are nothing but endless.
Just trust in her heart and she will overcome those broken promises.

Zeeni M

She commands the microphone with ease.
Her ultimate goal is for the crowd to please.
Filling the air with a joyful rapture.
She works the crowd with her therapy of laughter.

Her name is Zeeni M, an entertainer of note.
She will leave you in stitches, sadness's special antidote.
A warm-hearted woman, that puts others first.
She will guarantee, from happiness you will never thirst.

My friend, my PRO and above all, my slave driver.
For every occasion, she makes sure, that I deliver.
With great appreciation, I send a message her way.
You are truly a Godsend, who challenges me come what may.

With a vision of reaching for the stars, she works tirelessly.
Yielding to nothing, she gets her results miraculously.
There is no task too big for her to handle.
You will find her in the darkest of tunnels holding onto a candle.

This Picturesque Masterpiece
(Inspired by Ekta Somera)

Inside a picture lies thousands of untold stories.
From the dusk of time to our present glories.
What can we take from a picturesque masterpiece?
Only poets and lyricists dare to transform it into a centrepiece.

As birds sing melodically as the sun sets.
It catches the attention of a guitarist as he rests.
Taking to this makeshift stage, he creates a new vibe.
Churning out music that's soothing and easy to describe.

A dancer's feet mystically join into this rhythm.
Giving her the courage to live out her dream.
The entire sight was captured by an artist passing by.
Allowing for the world to see through his mind's eye.

Natural Light

No switch was required to turn on heaven's lights outside.
It was clear that from the brightness of the sun, no one could hide.
The air conditioner brought me some comfort from the heat
As I lifted my head from my book, I was greeted by a smile so sweet.

Her subtle beauty took my breath away,
And from her blue eyes, I was not able to stray.
Though she sat across the room, I felt her breathe upon my cheek.
My imagination was on a fuzz, and I felt like a freak.

I lowered my gaze and went on with my work.
I did not want to make her think that I was a jerk.
As I left my head, I noticed that she was looking at me.
So, I smiled back at her, not knowing how things would be.

Without waiting for an invite, I walked on over.
Stuck out my hand and said can I be your four-leaf clover.
A fascinating way for you to break the ice.
To offer to be my lucky charm, however, it sounds quite nice.

We spoke for a while, then exchanged our numbers.
Hoping to see each other through all our summers.
This was the only time she was present in this place.
So, we promised to stay friends with God's heavenly Grace.

My Special Peeps

Down by the ocean, down by the sea.
That's where you will find Ismail and Zee.
Making sandcastles with their buckets and spades.
Hoping that with the tide it does not fade.

He tugged at her hair, making her cry.
In a fit of anger, she threw sand in his eye.
I wish that, this was how their story began.
When she was the ying to his yang.

Reality will one day in the future unfold.
When their love story, I will finally get a hold.
Unlocking the lives of my special peeps.
The one's in my heart I will forever keep.
With great appreciation, I hold them dear.
May their lives be blessed, and their parts remain clear.

As their journey progress, keep them strong in mind.
May the path to each other, they will always find.
Give them the wisdom to fix when things go wrong.
Bless their hearts and keep their love forever strong.

Lonesome

On a rooftop stands a tormented soul.
From whom, life's lessons have eaten him whole.
He aimlessly gazes at the people bustling around the city.
Not really in search of anyone's pity.

A smile painted on his face as he sat there watching.
Alone he stands, whilst his next steps he is planning.
With an open mind, he envisions his future.
With a clear understanding of how to manoeuvre.

He sits all alone, escaping all pressure.
Relaxing his mind and creating a clearer picture.
For the path ahead he needs a positive mindset.
So that from his actions he bears no regret.

Though his journey seems lonesome, minus the pain.
It is the only path he knows that will make him whole again.
The losses he encountered, have dealt a heavy blow.
As he leaves his past behind, for a future
That will make him grow

History

I thought learning about the past was pretty cool.
So, I ended up studying history back in school.
The ways of the world and how things were done
Surpassing all wars and how humanity was won.

How our forefathers' struggles paved our way.
Giving us a direction to better our lives, come what may.
History books do not share all the fights they endured.
Nor of the countless lives they had to keep secure.

As their stories that were hidden come to be told.
Of sacrifices that were made whilst standing true and bold.
We pay homage to their tenacity as they stood firm in their fight.
Never for a moment afraid to die for what they knew was right.

We salute you our warriors who stood firm and strong.
Showing us that as rainbow a nation, we can overcome all wrong.
So, let's take heed of their call to leave a legacy behind.
So that new hope for our country the next generation will find

Hearts Strings

Cherished memories hold our heartsstrings together.
Giving us the strength to embrace a new day.
From the loss of loved ones, the pain lingers forever.
Creating a platform, so that love never goes away.

As good days draw near, old memories come flooding back.
Finding ourselves vulnerable and immune to new happiness.
The losses incurred take us off our track.
Reminding us of our loved ones, whilst bringing nothing but sadness.

As good days draw near, old memories come flooding back.
Leaving our hearts immune to new happiness.
For the loss incurred knocks us off our track.
With reminders of loved ones and nothing but sadness.

Four Seasons

We watch in springtime as Mother Nature is in motion.
Summoning her fairies to spread their magic potion.
As pixie dust is spread across the fields creating magic.
Listening to children's stories makes us all the more nostalgic.

With summer comes longer days for the children to play.
As the heat directs kids to the rivers and lakes come what may.
The joy that is spread as they run around carefree.
Enjoying every moment as kids should be.

Now autumn is the time when leaves start to fall.
Preparing in our minds for the changes as bare trees stand tall.
Like carpets, the leave covers the ground.
Creating nourishment and protection as winter comes around.

When the coldness of the winter finally makes its way.
Indoors under blankets is where the majority choose to stay.
The benefits of winter allow for growth and rest.
It nourishes the soil so that in spring the plants' growth is the best.

Apple of my Eye

My heart was a flutter, I knew not what to do.
As my mind started to wander, with thoughts of you.
Would I scare her away if I walked up to her?
I thought hard but considered trying later.

I felt it best to sit back and analyse the situation.
Whilst carefully planning my next action.
The last thing I wanted was to scare her away.
I knew that no matter what I would make progress today.

Something about her stood out for me.
Attracting my emotions, setting my thoughts free.
I knew that I had only one thing left to do.
To get up from my seat and make a positive breakthrough.

With the confidence gained, I walked to where she sat alone.
I saw you alone and I came over to chat.
I am no stalker, nor am I a creep.
I will gladly leave you be, a promise I will keep.

We sat there for a while as I learnt more of who she is.
Sharing our stories, with so much of ease.
We exchanged numbers that day, as we said our goodbyes.
She is still today, the apple of my eye.

Angelic Goddess
(Written for Shay Ramji)

Wrapped in her traditional garments wearing it with pride.
This beautiful young lady showed us her elegant side.
She was brimming with pleasure to unleash her heritage.
And openly smiled as she walked onto the stage.

As the music began, she gracefully swayed.
Smiling all the time as the music played.
When she started to sing, we were captivated by her voice.
This angelic goddess has managed to drown out all the noise.

Her voice was magical, and it beautified the beat.
The song that she sang had me tapping my feet.
I did not know the meaning of the lyrics of the song.
It would have mattered not, even if she said something wrong.

People got up and started dancing in the aisle.
I just sat there listening and smiling all the while.
For some reason, I kid you not, they were calling her Mausi.
But to me, she will always be the angelic Shay Ramji.

Rejuvenated

Sitting here under this tree, I feel no heat.
The coolness from the wind was a welcoming treat.
I was in no hurry, to move from this spot.
Away from the shade, the sun was blazing hot.

I removed my shoes and lay down on my back.
Resting my head, on my little knapsack.
I closed my eyes, as the wind blew through my hair.
In appreciation for the coolness, that greeted me there.

Without a care in the world, I rested my mind.
For both coolness and quietness, it was hard to find.
As minutes turned to hours, I remained in the shade.
Knowing full well that it was a wise choice I had made.

Grabbing my stuff, I got back to my feet.
With the sun setting, I was back out on the street.
Homeward bound, feeling rejuvenated.
Not thinking for a moment of the time that was wasted.

New Opportunities

In search of new opportunities, I take on the open road.
With the utmost of self-confidence, I abandoned my humble abode.
The journey ahead looks somewhat lonesome.
But my beating heart is filled with energised enthusiasm.

As the tar lays invitingly beneath my feet,
I look ahead as I strap on to the seat.
Foot on the gas, I head off to an unplanned destination.
Eager to explore what lies ahead without any hesitation.

I roll down the window, enjoying the cool breeze.
Chuffed with myself for doing as I please.
With no trouble on my mind, I was finally on my way.
Knowing full well that I will achieve my goal someday.

Looking out at the open road I felt so much at ease.
I finally convinced myself at this moment to cease.
I was thankful for the courage that sparked this trip.
For my future is mine and I will hold it with a firm grip.

New Mindset

Battle-scarred, wearily he drags himself across the sand.
With a brave heart, he trudges through a foreign land.
In search of a sanctuary from the scars, he chooses to hide.
With a new determination to succeed, he widens his stride.

Stepping into a bar, he knew full well.
That from this new adventure he cannot kiss and tell.
His mind was at ease as he sipped on his drink.
Smiling as he looked around managing to catch a wink.

Sitting at the bar, this sultry lady was such a looker.
Later in time, he found out that she was just a hooker.
The deed was done, he released all tension.
This is one of those stories knowing full well not to mention
.
With head held high, and a skip in his step.
He made his way home, with a new mindset.
From here on out, he will not lose sleep.
Living his best life, with a healthy sanity to keep.

New Beginnings

Behind closed doors, she hides her tears.
Wanting not unto others, to disclose her fears.
Lost in her world she is happy to be alone.
The path that she chose is from her mistakes to atone.

With a newfound zest for life, she left the city.
Never looking back or accepting anyone's pity.
From her past mistakes, she dares not hide.
With head held high, she takes everything in her stride.

As she opens the door to a whole new beginning.
Joyful songs in her head she is already singing.
As she gazes upon this beautiful new day.
Filling her heart in a positive way.
Holding nothing back, she pushes through.
Forging new bonds in search of new things to do.

My Kryptonite

A shiver ran down my spine, as she came into sight.
I cannot explain it, but she was definitely my kryptonite.
A simplistic young lady, a diamond in the rough.
I tried to move away but learned I was not fast enough.

As she slowly made her way into the room.
The aura around her was like a rose in full bloom.
I could feel my heart beating inside my head.
Both my feet planted as though they were filled with lead.

I smelt the sweet fragrance from her perfume as she came closer.
I prayed for strength not to crumble under this pressure.
My prayers were in vain as she stopped in front of me.
My heart stopped beating as she whispered, long time no see.

My face was hot and as white as snow.
And like a rabbit in the headlights, I had nowhere to go.
I watched as a smile traced her beautiful face.
Without waiting for a response, she turned and went to her place.

I hated how she made me feel.
Lost in a stupor, with this weakness I must deal.
Before the night could come to an end.
I made her aware, that from her pain I will mend.

May

May the light from our hearts shine ever so bright.
May the wind in our sails keep the horizons in our sight.
May the tears from heaven bring life to this land.
May the flowers be the anchor of salvation in the sand.

May the warmth of the sun melt our hearts of ice.
May the goodness in our hearts bring all things nice.
May the fire within us burn strong for eternity.
May all mothers bring to life a child's purity.

May the heaven look down upon us with favour.
May we be blessed with the strength not to waver.
May the trumpets blast bring nothing but honour.
May we be ever grateful for the love from our saviour.

May we look back on life and respect all religions, creed and colour.
May we be forever forgiving of one another.
May we never allow greed to swallow us whole.
May we set an example for future leaders to reach for that one goal.

Life's Mistakes

Into my shell for now I choose to slowly retreat.
Away from unwanted noise, I will find myself a seat.
Alone I will take time to recap on what went wrong.
Reassessing my life, and where I belong.

I will drown out all the noise that messed with my mind.
I will search deep within for the answers I hope I find.
I had ignored the obvious that was in plain sight.
But the time has come for me to get my perspective right.

It's time to hit rewind, reboot and most of all reset.
If only life's mistakes were that easy to forget.
With a positive mindset, I'm leaving my mistakes behind.
As I go in search of new beginnings and a peaceful mind.

Dreams I Dream

I'm lost in dreams as I look at you.
Hoping they can be transformed into something true.
If I could get lost in your beauty, right here in this place.
I would sit here for hours, just staring at your face.

If only I could space out in time, lost in your baby blue eyes.
Or sitting here in your company, watching as time flies.
If only I could hold you close and feel the beating of your heart.
Or admire your outer beauty like a priceless work of art.

These dreams I dream, as I look at you.
If only you were mine, those dreams would come true.
But like all dreams, one needs to wake.
And the cruelty of life is all I get to take.

Christmas Spark

The festive season is unloaded as December is finally here.
Excited people shopping, spending with little care.
In search of fancy clothing, on Christmas for them to wear.
Some are in search of special gifts, with loved ones they can share.

Children waiting patiently, with the greatest of anticipation.
For the good they have done, a present being their only expectation.
Adults do their best to keep the children guessing.
That on Christmas day, a toy, Santa will be bringing.

There are those that support the poor, by sharing with them their gifts.
Opening up their hearts, in true humanitarian spirits.
Searching for ways to ignite, a magical Christmas spark
These angels bring into the light, those left out in the dark.

Christmas parties are being prepared with just one call.
So that all of God's creation can have a Christmas ball.
May the spirit of Christmas remind us of the joyous tidings.
Let's release all the love from wherever they may be hiding.
Show strength as the world is going through a rebirth.
Let's celebrate Christmas as one, as we rebuild our earth.

A New Day

Washed away by the rain are the problems of yesterday.
Let's start afresh with appreciation of a new day.
Those problems that you allowed to weigh you down.
If not controlled will someday cause you to drown.

As the sun shines brightly bringing warmth to all.
May we take blessings from the sun's rays that fall on us.
Let the heat warm our hearts and keep us where we belong.
Like the sunflowers facing the sun standing ever so strong.

As we embrace each new day, let's work as a team.
Supporting each other in achieving our dreams.
For the one thing that a new day has taught.
Not many people get to see a new day come forth.

www.ingramcontent.com/pod-product-compliance
Lightning Source LLC
Chambersburg PA
CBHW062052290426
44109CB00027B/2806